United States
Department of
Agriculture
Food and
Nutrition
Service

Accommodating Children with Special Dietary Needs in the School Nutrition Programs

Guidance for School Food Service Staff

In accordance with Federal law and U.S. Department of Agriculture policy, this institution is prohibited from discriminating on the basis of race, color, national origin, sex, age or disability.

To file a complaint of discrimination, write USDA, Director, Office of Civil Rights, Room 326-W, Whitten Building, 1400 Independence Avenue, SW, Washington, D.C., 20250-9410, or call 202-720-5964 (voice and TDD). USDA is an equal opportunity provider and employer.

No substantive changes were made to this manual. Minor updates were made and several obsolete appendices were deleted.

Fall 2001

GUIDANCE FOR ACCOMMODATING CHILDREN
WITH SPECIAL DIETARY NEEDS
IN THE SCHOOL NUTRITION PROGRAMS

TABLE OF CONTENTS

LIST OF APPENDICES

GUIDANCE FOR ACCOMMODATING CHILDREN
WITH SPECIAL DIETARY NEEDS
IN THE SCHOOL NUTRITION PROGRAMS

I.   INTRODUCTION

In recent years, we have seen increasing emphasis on the importance of ensuring that children with disabilities have the same opportunities as other children to receive an education and education-related benefits, such as school meals.

Congress first addressed this concern in *The Rehabilitation Act of 1973*, which prohibits discrimination against qualified persons with disabilities in the programs or activities of any agency of the federal government's executive branch or any organization receiving federal financial assistance.

Subsequently, Congress passed the *Education of the Handicapped Act*, (now, the *Individuals with Disabilities Education Act*), which requires that a free and appropriate public education be provided for children with disabilities, who are aged 3 through 21, and the *Americans with Disabilities Act*, a comprehensive law which broadens and extends civil rights protections for Americans with disabilities.

One effect of these laws has been an increase in the number of children with disabilities who are being educated in regular school programs. In some cases, the disability may prevent the child from eating meals prepared for the general school population.

The U.S. Department of Agriculture's (USDA) nondiscrimination regulation (7 CFR 15b), as well as the regulations governing the National School Lunch Program and School Breakfast Program, make it clear that substitutions to the regular meal must be made for children who are unable to eat school meals because of their disabilities, when that need is certified by a licensed physician.

In most cases, children with disabilities can be accommodated with little extra expense or involvement. The nature of the child's disability, the reason the disability prevents the child from eating the regular school meal, and the specific substitutions needed must be specified in a statement signed by a licensed physician. Often, the substitutions can be made relatively easily. There are situations, however, which may require additional equipment or specific technical training and expertise. When these instances occur, it is important that school food service managers and parent(s) be involved at the outset in preparations for the child's entrance into the school.

This guidance describes some of the factors which must be considered in the early phases of planning and suggests ways in which the school food service can interact with other responsible parties in the school and the community at large to serve children with disabilities.

The guidance is based on the policy guidelines outlined in the FNS Instruction 783-2, Revision 2, *Meal Substitutions for Medical or Other Special Dietary Reasons.*

Serving children with disabilities presents school food service staff with new challenges as well as rewards. This guidance presents information on how to handle situations that may arise and offers advice about such issues as funding and liability.

The guidance was prepared in consultation with the U.S. Department of Justice and the U.S. Department of Education and will be periodically updated to reflect new scientific information or new statutory and program guidelines.

II. DEFINITIONS OF DISABILITY AND OF OTHER SPECIAL DIETARY NEEDS

A. DISABILITY

Rehabilitation Act of 1973 and the *Americans with Disabilities Act*

Under Section 504 of the *Rehabilitation Act of 1973,* and the *Americans with Disabilities Act* (ADA) of 1990, a "person with a disability" means any person who has a physical or mental impairment which substantially limits one or more major life activities, has a record of such an impairment, or is regarded as having such an impairment.

The term "physical or mental impairment" includes many diseases and conditions, a few of which may be:

- orthopedic, visual, speech, and hearing impairments;
- cerebral palsy;
- epilepsy;
- muscular dystrophy;
- multiple sclerosis;
- cancer;
- heart disease;
- metabolic diseases, such as diabetes or phenylketonuria (PKU);
- food anaphylaxis (severe food allergy);
- mental retardation;
- emotional illness;
- drug addiction and alcoholism;
- specific learning disabilities;
- HIV disease; and
- tuberculosis.

Please refer to the Acts noted above for a more detailed explanation.

Major life activities covered by this definition include caring for one's self, eating, performing manual tasks, walking, seeing, hearing, speaking, breathing, learning, and working.

Individuals with Disabilities Education Act

The term child with a "disability" under Part B of the *Individuals with Disabilities Education Act* (IDEA) means a child evaluated in accordance with IDEA as having one or more of the recognized thirteen disability categories and who, by reason thereof, needs special education and related services.

IDEA recognizes thirteen disability categories which establish a child's need for special education and related services. These disabilities include:

- autism;
- deaf-blindness;
- deafness or other hearing impairments;
- mental retardation;
- orthopedic impairments;
- other health impairments due to chronic or acute health problems, such as asthma, diabetes, nephritis, sickle cell anemia, a heart condition, epilepsy, rheumatic fever, hemophilia, leukemia, lead poisoning, tuberculosis;
- emotional disturbance;
- specific learning disabilities;
- speech or language impairment;
- traumatic brain injury; and
- visual impairment; including blindness which adversely affects a child's educational performance, and
- multiple disabilities.

Attention deficit disorder or attention deficit hyperactivity disorder may fall under one of the thirteen categories. Classification depends upon the particular characteristics associated with the disorder and how the condition manifests itself in the student, which will determine the category.

The Individualized Education Program or IEP means a written statement for a child with a disability that is developed, reviewed, and revised in accordance with the IDEA and its implementing regulations. The IEP is the cornerstone of the student's educational program that contains the program of special education and related services to be provided to a child with a disability covered under the IDEA.

NOTE: Some states supplement the IEP with a written statement specifically designed to address a student's nutritional needs. Other states employ a "Health Care Plan" to address the nutritional needs of their students. For ease of reference, the term "IEP" is used to reflect the IEP as well as any written statement designating the required nutrition services.

When nutrition services are required under a child's IEP, school officials need to make sure that school food service staff are involved early on in decisions regarding special meals.

Physician's Statement for Children with Disabilities

USDA regulations 7 CFR Part 15b require substitutions or modifications in school meals for children whose disabilities restrict their diets. A child with a disability must be provided substitutions in foods when that need is supported by a statement signed by a licensed physician. The physician's statement must identify:

✓ the child's disability;
✓ an explanation of why the disability restricts the child's diet;
✓ the major life activity affected by the disability;
✓ the food or foods to be omitted from the child's diet, and the food or choice of foods that must be substituted.

In Cases of Food Allergy

Generally, children with food allergies or intolerances do not have a disability as defined under either Section 504 of the Rehabilitation Act or Part B of IDEA, and the school food service may, but is not required to, make food substitutions for them.

However, when in the licensed physician's assessment, food allergies may result in severe, life-threatening (anaphylactic) reactions, the child's condition would meet the definition of "disability," and the substitutions prescribed by the licensed physician must be made.

B.   OTHER SPECIAL DIETARY NEEDS

The school food service may make food substitutions, at their discretion, for individual children who do not have a disability, but who are medically certified as having a special medical or dietary need.

Such determinations are only made on a case-by-case basis. This provision covers those children who have food intolerances or allergies but do not have life-threatening reactions (anaphylactic reactions) when exposed to the food(s) to which they have problems.

Medical Statement for Children with Special Dietary Needs

Each special dietary request must be supported by a statement, which explains the food substitution that is requested. It must be signed by a recognized medical authority.

The medical statement must include:

✓   an identification of the medical or other special dietary condition which restricts the child's diet;
✓   the food or foods to be omitted from the child's diet; and
✓   the food or choice of foods to be substituted.

III. SCHOOL ISSUES

The school food service, like the other programs in the school, is responsible for ensuring that its benefits (meals) are made available to all children, including children with disabilities. This raises questions in a number of areas:

A.   What are the responsibilities of the school food service?

B.   Where can additional funds be obtained?

C.   Who can provide more information and technical assistance?

A.   SCHOOL FOOD SERVICE RESPONSIBILITIES

✓   School food service staff must make food substitutions or modifications for students with disabilities.

✓   Substitutions or modifications for children with disabilities must be based on a prescription written by a licensed physician.

✓   The school food service is encouraged, but not required, to provide food substitutions or modifications for children without disabilities with medically certified special dietary needs who are unable to eat regular meals as prepared.

✓   Substitutions for children without disabilities, with medically certified special dietary needs must be based on a statement by a recognized medical authority.

✓   Under no circumstances are school food service staff to revise or change a diet prescription or medical order.

✓   For USDA's basic guidelines on meal substitutions and accessibility, see FNS Instruction 783-2, Revision 2, *Meal Substitutions for Medical or Other Special Dietary Reasons*, in **Appendix A**.

✓   It is important that all recommendations for accommodations or changes to existing diet orders be documented in writing to protect the school and minimize misunderstandings. Schools should retain copies of special, non-meal pattern diets on file for reviews.

✓   The diet orders do not need to be renewed on a yearly basis; however schools are encouraged to ensure that the diet orders reflect the current dietary needs of the child.

Providing Special Meals to Children with Disabilities

The school food service is required to offer special meals, at no additional cost, to children whose disability restricts their diet as defined in USDA's nondiscrimination regulations, 7 CFR Part 15b.

✓   If a child's IEP includes a nutrition component, the school should ensure that school food service managers are involved early on in decisions regarding special meals or modifications.

✓   The school food service is not required to provide meal services to children with disabilities when the meal service is not normally available to the general student body, unless a meal service is required under the child's IEP.

For example, if a school breakfast program is not offered, the school food service is not required to provide breakfast to the child with a disability, unless this is specified in the child's IEP.

However, if a student is receiving special education and has an IEP, and the IEP indicates that the child needs to be served breakfast at school, then the school is required to provide this meal to the child and may choose to have the school food service handle the responsibility. This is discussed in more detail in *Section V*, under Situation 2.

Menu Modifications for Children with Disabilities

Children with disabilities who require changes to the basic meal (such as special supplements or substitutions) are required to provide documentation with accompanying instructions from a licensed physician.

This is required to ensure that the modified meal is reimbursable, and to ensure that any meal modifications meet nutrition standards which are medically appropriate for the child.

Texture Modifications for Children with Disabilities

For children with disabilities who only require modifications in texture (such as chopped, ground or pureed foods), a licensed physician's written instructions indicating the appropriate food texture is recommended, but not required.

However, the State agency or school food authority may apply stricter guidelines, and require that the school keep on file a licensed physician's statement concerning needed modifications in food texture.

✓ In order to minimize the chance of misunderstandings, it is recommended that the school food service, at a minimum, maintain written instructions or guidance from a licensed physician regarding the texture modifications to be made. For children receiving special education, the texture modification should be included in the IEP.

✓ School food service staff must follow the instructions that have been prescribed by the licensed physician.

Serving the Special Dietary Needs of Children Without Disabilities

Children without disabilities, but with special dietary needs requiring food substitutions or modifications, may request that the school food service meet their special nutrition needs.

✓ The school food authority will decide these situations on a case-by-case basis. Documentation with accompanying information must be provided by a recognized medical authority.

✓ While school food authorities are encouraged to consult with recognized medical authorities, where appropriate, schools are not required to make modifications to meals based on food choices of a family or child regarding a healthful diet.

B.   FUNDING SOURCES

Price of Meals

Meals must be served free or at a reduced price (a maximum of 40 cents for lunch and 30 cents for breakfast) to children who qualify for these benefits regardless of whether or not they have a disability.

Schools may not charge children with disabilities or with certified special dietary needs who require food substitutions or modifications more than they charge other children for program meals or snacks.

Incurring Additional Expenses

In most cases, children with disabilities can be accommodated with little extra expense or involvement. If additional expenses are incurred in providing food substitutions or modifications for children with special needs, generally the school food authority should be able to absorb the cost of making meal modifications or paying for the services of a registered dietician.

However, when the school food service has difficulty covering the additional cost, there are several alternative sources of funding which school food service managers, school administrators, parents or guardians, and teachers may consider. These sources include the school district's general fund and the additional funding sources listed below.

Any additional funding received by school food services for costs incurred in providing special meals must accrue to the nonprofit school food service account.

POTENTIAL FUNDING SOURCES

Individuals with Disabilities Education Act

The *Individuals with Disabilities Education Act* (IDEA), through the Part B Program, provides Federal funds to assist States and school districts in making a **"free appropriate public education"** available to eligible children with specified disabilities residing within the State.

Students with specified physical, mental, emotional or sensory impairments that need special education and related services are eligible for services under IDEA, **at no cost to parents.**

In appropriate situations, nutrition services may be specified as **special education** (specially designed instruction) or a **related service** (support services required to assist a child with a disability to benefit from special education).

Services which may be funded through IDEA include: (1) purchase of special foods, supplements, or feeding equipment; (2) consultation services of a registered dietitian or nutrition professional; and (3) assistance of a special education teacher, occupational therapist or other health professional in feeding the child or developing feeding skills.

Website address: Department of Education/IDEA: http://www.ed.gov, (scroll down to "Most Requested Items" Disabilities Education (IDEA))

Medicaid

Title XIX of the *Social Security Act* is an entitlement program which finances medical services for certain individuals and families with low income and resources.

Within broad Federal guidelines, a State or territory: (1) establishes its own eligibility standards; (2) determines the type, amount, duration, and scope of services; (3) sets the rates of payment for services; and (4) administers its own program.

The Medicaid program, jointly funded by Federal and State governments, varies considerably from State to State as each State adapts the program to its own unique environment.

In the case of certain low-income children eligible for Medicaid, Medicaid may pay for services that are medical and remedial in nature. These services may include special dietary supplements, eating devices, and nutritional consultation as medically necessary.

Medicaid reimbursement is paid directly to the provider of services, such as a physician, pharmacy, medical equipment supplier, clinic, and, in certain situations, the school food authority and/or school. Questions regarding provider qualifications should be directed to your State Medicaid agency.

If you have questions about who has access to Medicaid, how to qualify as an authorized provider, or what services are covered by Medicaid in your State, contact your State Medicaid agency.

For information or a referral, check with the Medicaid division, at the regional office of the Health Care Financing Administration for your State. (See **Appendix C)**

Website address: http://www.hcfa.gov/medicaid/.

Early and Periodic Screening, Diagnostic and Treatment Program

Medicaid's child health program, the Early and Periodic Screening, Diagnostic and Treatment (EPSDT) Program is a preventive and comprehensive health care benefit for Medicaid-eligible individuals up to age 21. EPSDT includes screening for dental, hearing and vision services. An objective of the EPSDT Program is to detect and treat health problems and conditions early before they become more complex and costly. The EPSDT Program allows providers, including schools, to be reimbursed for preventive and treatment services for Medicaid-eligible children. Questions regarding EPSDT coverage under Medicaid should be directed to the State Medicaid agency or to your State EPSDT Coordinator.

Website address: http://www.hcfa.gov/medicaid/EPSDThm.htm

Supplemental Security Income

Supplemental Security Income (SSI), under Title V of the *Social Security Act*, provides rehabilitative services to children under age 16 who are receiving benefits under SSI, to the extent that Medicaid does not cover the service. SSI provides basic income for needy children under age 18 (students under age 22) who are blind or who have a severe disability or chronic illness.

For information on SSI eligibility, contact your local Social Security Office or call the Social Security Administration's toll free telephone number, 1-800-772-1213, (TTY/TDD, 1-800-325-0778).

Website address: http://www.SSA.gov, and scroll down to Supplemental Security Income

Medicare

Medicare provides services for children and adults with end-stage renal (kidney) disease. However, Medicare coverage of nutritional supplies is generally limited to durable medical equipment such as a feeding pump or other special (parenteral or enteral) nutritional feeding equipment necessary for people who cannot be sustained through normal means of feeding by mouth.

For more information, telephone the toll free Medicare Hotline at, 1-800-633-4227 or (TTY/TDD, 1-800-820-1202).

Website address: http://www.medicare.gov

Maternal and Child Health (MCH) Services Block Grants

The Maternal and Child Health Bureau, at the Department of Health and Human Services, administers Maternal and Child Health Services Block Grants, authorized under Title V of the *Social Security Act*. These grants enable States to assess health needs and provide a wide range of community-based services for children with special health care needs.

State Title V programs work closely with community health centers, public health clinics, and school health programs. Contact the Regional MCH Program Consultant for your State, listed in **Appendix C**, for information about your State's Title V program activities.

Community Sources

Parent Teacher Associations (PTA), voluntary health associations, local civic organizations, and other community-based groups may be able to assist with the procurement of equipment and provide other support services. See **Appendix D** for a partial list of voluntary and professional health organizations which offer information and support for various disabilities or special health care needs.

C.   HELPFUL RESOURCES

School food service staff should work closely with the support people who are familiar with the needs of the child. The child's parents or guardians, teachers, occupational and physical therapists, special education staff, and the school nurse are valuable resources.

Local health department, hospital, or medical center registered dietitians may be able to provide assistance in understanding diet orders, developing and modifying meal plans and menus, special food item purchases, and other aspects of feeding children with special needs.

In addition, the following resources may provide technical assistance or referrals to qualified nutrition and health professionals:

- **State Title V Directors, Maternal and Child Health (MCH)**
Each State has a Title V director responsible for overseeing State programs for children with special health care needs. Most States also have public health nutritionists who are responsible for nutritional services for these children.

Contact the Regional MCH Program Consultant for your State listed in Appendix C for information on State Title V program activities or refer to your State Title V MCH personnel.

- **Registered Dietitians of the American Dietetic Association (ADA)**

Registered Dietitians (R.D.) can answer questions on special diets and menu planning to help school food service staff better understand a child's special dietary needs. An R.D. may work with the recognized medical authority and the school food service to help meet a child's special nutritional needs and ensure that menus comply with the diet order. These types of services are allowable program costs.

The ADA's toll free Consumer Nutrition Information/Hotline is 1-800-366-1655 which can provide referrals to qualified R.D.s in your area as well as daily nutrition messages.

Website address: http://www.eatright.org

- **University Affiliated Programs for Developmentally Disabled (UAP)**

UAPs were established to support the independence, productivity, and community integration of all citizens with developmental disabilities.

Within their States, UAPs serve as links between the academic world and the delivery of services to persons with developmental disabilities. UAPS also provide families and individuals with a variety of support services.

For a referral to a UAP in your area, contact the National Office of the American Association of University Affiliated Programs at (301) 588-8252.

Website address: http://www.aauap.org

- **Regional Disability and Business Technical Assistance Centers**

Ten regional centers are funded by the National Institute on Disability Rehabilitation and Research of the U.S. Department of Education to provide information and technical assistance on the Americans with Disabilities Act (ADA). The Regional ADA Coalition in your area may also be helpful.

Copies of ADA documents, supplied by the Equal Employment Opportunity Commission and the Department of Justice, may be obtained at any of the regional centers. These materials are available in standard print, large print, Braille, on audiocassette and computer disk.

For the telephone number and address of your regional center, call the ADA Technical Assistance Center's toll free number: 1-800-949-4ADA.

• **Other Health Care and Disability Related Organizations**
Appendix D contains a listing of organizations which may offer assistance regarding children with different health care needs. The appendix includes such organizations as the American Diabetes Association, the Food Allergy and Anaphylaxis Network, United Cerebral Palsy
Association, the Easter Seal Society, and many more.

D.   INFORMATION SOURCES

There are a growing number of excellent information services that can provide resources and answer your questions about accommodating children with special dietary needs.

The following are federally funded sources:

• **Food and Nutrition Information Center** (FNIC).
FNIC is an information center located at USDA's National Agricultural Library (NAL). FNIC staff has prepared resource lists on food service topics that are located on their website. Phone FNIC for more information. (301) 504-5719, or TTY: (301) 504-6856).

Website address: http://www.nal.usda.gov/fnic.

FNIC's Healthy School Meals Resource System offers online training materials and connects with other food service resources.

Website address: http://schoolmeals.nal.usda.gov

- **National Agriculture Library (NAL)**

NAL has a large collection of books, videos, teaching kits, professional journals and other library resources on food and nutrition topics. Phone NAL for more information. (301) 504-5755.

Website address: http://www.nal.usda.gov

- **National Food Service Management Institute (NFSMI), University of Mississippi**

NFSMI at the University of Mississippi is a national resource for the child nutrition programs. It provides information services and referral in all areas of nutrition and school food service. NFSMI staff can give practical answers to question regarding serving children with special nutritional needs. Call the Help Desk at 1-800-321-3054, or (662) 915-7658.

Website address: http://www.nfsmi.org.

- **National Information Center for Children and Youth with Disabilities (NICHCY)**

NICHCY is an information and referral center for children with disabilities and disability related issues which receives funding through the U.S. Department of Education. Information specialists provide information in English and Spanish regarding services about specific disabilities, special education and related services, education programs, family issues or disability organizations. The toll free number is 1-800-695-0285.

NICHCY staff has prepared State Resource Sheets for each State which can be downloaded from its web site. The resource sheet for your State will help you locate government agencies, chapters of disability organizations, parent training and information projects. The resource sheet can also refer you to local sources of information and assistance.

Website address: http://www.nichcy.org

IV. LEGAL CONCERNS AND LIABILITY IN WORKING WITH CHILDREN WITH DISABILITES

A growing body of Federal law clearly intends that children with disabilities have the same rights and privileges, and the same access to benefits, such as school meals, as children without disabilities. Consequently, schools which do not make appropriate program accommodations for children with disabilities, could be found in violation of Federal civil rights laws.

School administrators and food service staff should be aware of two issues involving liability: (1) the school's responsibility for providing program accommodations for children with disabilities and (2) the question of personal responsibility in cases of negligence. These two issues are discussed below.

A. SCHOOL RESPONSIBILITY TO MAKE ACCOMMODATIONS

Section 504
Rehabilitation Act of 1973

Section 504 of the *Rehabilitation Act of 1973* specifically mandates that:

> "no otherwise qualified individual with a disability shall solely by reason of his or her disability be excluded from the participation in, be denied the benefits of, or be subjected to discrimination under any program or activity receiving Federal financial assistance."

This mandate is incorporated in 7 CFR Part 15b, USDA's nondiscrimination regulations.

Individuals with Disabilities Education Act

Part B of the *Individuals with Disabilities Education Act (IDEA)* assists States and school districts in making a **"free appropriate public education"** available to eligible students.

Under IDEA, a "free appropriate public education" means special education and related services provided under public supervision and direction in conformity with an individualized education program (IEP) at no cost to parents.

In appropriate situations, nutrition services could be considered "special education" (specially designed instruction) or a "related service", (support services required to assist a child with a disability to benefit from special education).

Title II
Americans With Disabilities Act
Title II of the *Americans with Disabilities Act* (ADA), enacted in 1990, requires equal availability and accessibility in State and local government programs and services, including public schools.

In this respect, the ADA underscores the statutory prohibition of Section 504 of the Rehabilitation Act of 1973, against discrimination on the basis of disability by programs receiving Federal funding, such as reimbursement under the school meal programs.

Title II of the ADA does not impose any major new requirements on school districts because the requirements of Title II and Section 504 are similar. Virtually all school districts receive Federal financial assistance and have been required to comply with Section 504 for many years.

Title III
Americans With Disabilities Act
Title III of the ADA extends requirements for public accommodations to privately owned facilities.

All private schools participating in the federally funded child nutrition programs must make accommodations to enable children with disabilities to receive school meals.

Although religious organizations are exempt from the public accommodations requirements of Title III, church-operated schools which receive Federal funding assistance under the child nutrition programs continue to be subject to the non-discrimination requirements of Section 504.

B.   PERSONAL RESPONSIBILITY IN CASES OF NEGLIGENCE

In order to accommodate a child with a disability, the school must ensure that both facilities and personnel are adequate to provide necessary services.

In some cases, it may be advisable for specially trained personnel, such as a registered dietitian to provide guidance to the school food service staff on how to modify a child's meals to comply with requirements as provided in the licensed physician's statement.

Moreover, for certain children with disabilities, it may be necessary to have a nurse or trained health aide feed the child or have a specially trained professional, such as a special education teacher, occupational therapist, or speech therapist, assist the child to develop and improve his or her eating skills.

Administering Feedings

For children requiring assistance in eating, the determination of who will feed the child is a local school decision.

While the school food service is specifically responsible for providing the necessary foods needed by a child with a disability, it is not the specific responsibility of the school food service staff to physically feed the child.

Furthermore, schools should be aware that they could be held liable if persons without sufficient training are performing tasks or activities such as developing or modifying a diet order prescribed by a licensed physician or administering tube feedings.

Diet Orders

If school food service staff have questions about the diet order, the prescribed meal substitutions, or any other modifications that are required, the child's physician and/or a registered dietitian should be consulted. If the school food service director cannot obtain local level assistance, the State agency should be consulted for technical assistance.

Under no circumstances should school food service staff diagnose health conditions, perform a nutritional assessment, prescribe nutritional requirements, or **interpret**, **revise** or **change** a diet order.

Negligence

If a mishap should occur, personal liability would normally depend on whether or not the person responsible for the feeding has been negligent.

In these cases, a determination that a person acted negligently would be made on the basis of State laws and the facts in the individual situation.

In general, negligence occurs when a person fails to exercise the care expected of a prudent person.

Persons involved with special feeding operations should, therefore, make sure that they thoroughly understand the required procedures and techniques and are careful to follow instructions.

For specific guidance concerning personal liability, the school officials should contact State or local legal counsel.

V.   SITUATIONS AND RESPONSES

In order to provide some practical guidelines, this section discusses several situations which are relatively common and which have raised questions in the past. These examples have been included because they illustrate certain principles and give general direction on what schools and institutions must do under the law. In all situations where a student's IEP indicates nutritional requirements or components, schools must make these accommodations.

Remember that circumstances vary from case to case. Schools should not automatically assume that the responses given in this section would always apply. When an actual situation occurs which has elements different from those discussed here, the State agency should be consulted for guidance.

The examples in this section have been grouped under the following topics:

- Meals and/or foods outside of the normal meal service
- Special needs which may or may not involve disabilities
- Responsibilities of food service management companies and other food service operations
- Feeding in separate facilities—generally not acceptable
- Temporary disabilities
- Complicated feedings
- School food service account and
- Documentation

A. MEALS AND/OR FOODS OUTSIDE OF THE NORMAL MEAL SERVICE

Situation 1:
As part of the therapy for a child with a disability, the licensed physician has required the child to consume six cans of cranberry juice a day. The juice is to be served at regular intervals, and some of these servings would occur outside of the normal school meal periods. Is the school food service required to provide all of the servings of juice?

Response:
No. The general guideline in making accommodations is that children with disabilities must be able to participate in and receive benefits from programs that are available to children without disabilities.

In this example, the school food service would be required to provide (and pay for) cranberry juice as part of the regular reimbursable breakfast, lunch and/or snack service. However, the school food service would not be required to pay for other servings throughout the school day <u>unless</u> specified in the Individualized Education Plan (IEP).

It must be recognized that there will be exceptions to this general rule. For example, residential child care institutions (RCCI), such as juvenile correction facilities, may be required to provide additional foods or servings since the child would have no other recourse for meals.

It must be stressed that such accommodation would depend on the specific circumstances of each case and, in any event, would go beyond obligations under the school nutrition programs.

In general, additional servings beyond what is required under the program meal may, but need not, be charged to the nonprofit food service account.

Situation 2:
A child with a disability must have a full breakfast each morning. Is the school food service required to provide a breakfast for this child even though a breakfast program is not available for the general school population?

Response:
As noted above, the school food service is not required to provide services and meals to children with disabilities that are not otherwise available to children who are not disabled. If the school does not have a breakfast program already, it does not need to initiate a program exclusively for children with disabilities.

However, if the IEP requires that a child receive a breakfast at school, the school must provide the service, and may choose to have the school food service handle the responsibility.

Another exception to the general rule concerns a child with a disability who resides in a RCCI and requires special food service. In the case of RCCIs, the institution serves as the child's home, and the child would have no other recourse for meals. The RCCI must provide the child a full breakfast, if this is specified in the licensed physician's statement or in the IEP.

Situation 3:
A licensed physician has prescribed portion sizes that exceed the minimum quantity requirements set forth in the regulations. Is the school required to provide these additional quantities?

Response:
Yes. The school must provide the child food portions which exceed the minimum quantity requirements, if specifically prescribed in the licensed physician's statement.

B. SPECIAL NEEDS WHICH MAY OR MAY NOT INVOLVE DISABILITIES

Situation 4:
A child has a life threatening allergy which causes an anaphylactic reaction to peanuts. The slightest contact with peanuts or peanut derivatives, usually peanut oil, could be fatal. To what lengths must the food service go to accommodate the child? Is it sufficient for the school food service to merely avoid obvious foods, such as peanut butter, or must school food service staff research every ingredient and additive in processed foods or regularly post all of the ingredients used in recipes?

Response:
The school has the responsibility to provide a safe, non-allergic meal to the child if it is determined that the condition is disabling. To do so, school food service staff must make sure that all food items offered to the allergic child meet prescribed guidelines and are free of foods which are suspected of causing the allergic reaction.

This means that the food labels or specifications will need to be checked to ensure that they do not contain traces of such substances. In some cases, the labels will provide enough information to make a reasonable judgment possible. If they do not provide enough information, it is the responsibility of the school food service to obtain the necessary information to ensure that no allergic substances are present in the foods served.

In some cases, it may be necessary to contact the supplier or the manufacturer or to check with the State agency. Private organizations, such as the Food Allergy and Anaphylaxis Network (see **Appendix D**), may also be consulted for information and advice. It is also wise to check with parents about certain foods and even provide them with advance copies of menus.

The general rule in these situations is to exercise caution at all times. Do not serve foods to children at risk for anaphylactic reactions, if you do not know what is in those foods. It is important to recognize that a child may be provided a meal, which is equivalent to the meal served to other children, but not necessarily the same meal.

Sometimes, it will be advisable to prepare a separate meal "from scratch" using ingredients that are allowed on the special diet rather than serving a meal using processed foods.

Situation 5:
A child has a health condition that does not meet the definition of "disability" set forth in the legislation and regulations. For example, the child is overweight (but not "morbidly" so), or the child has elevated blood cholesterol. Is the school obligated to accommodate the special dietary needs of this child?

Response:
The school may make substitutions for children who are not considered to be disabled, but who should avoid certain foods. However, the school is not required to do so. When the school does elect to accommodate children without disabilities, it must have a supporting statement, signed by a recognized medical authority on file.

In most cases, the dietary needs of such children can be accommodated at the food service site in schools and institutions where a variety of nutritious foods are available for individual choice. In addition, the "offer versus serve" provision which allows students the option to decline one or two foods in the normal (reimbursable) school meal may be of assistance in accommodating an individual's particular diet.

Situation 6:
A child's parents have requested that the school prepare a strict vegetarian diet for their child based on a statement from a health food store "nutrition advisor" who is not a licensed physician. Must the school comply with this request?

Response:
No. The school is responsible only for accommodating those conditions meeting the definition of disability as described in 7 CFR Part 15b. Schools are not required to make food substitutions based on food choices of a family or child regarding a healthful diet.

C. RESPONSIBILITIES OF FOOD SERVICE MANAGEMENT COMPANIES (FSMC) AND OTHER FOOD SERVICE OPERATIONS

Situation 7:
A school district has contracted with a FSMC to operate the school's food service. Is the FSMC obligated to accommodate children with disabilities?

Response:
Yes. The school is always required to ensure that any benefits available for the general school population are equally available to children with disabilities. Consequently, accommodations for these children must be made regardless of whether the school district operates the food service itself or contracts with an FSMC to do so.

However, as a procurement issue, accommodations for children with disabilities must be included in the contract. School food authorities that do not have any need for special dietary accommodations at the time a FSMC bid is prepared should still include sufficient information in the bid to ensure that the FSMC is aware that dietary accommodations may be required during the term of the contract.

Situation 8:
Some schools purchase items from nationally recognized fast-food chains and sell these items on an "a la carte" basis. These items are frequently sold in a setting such as a kiosk which uses the chain's logo or otherwise advertises the product. What obligation, if any, does the fast-food chain have to provide alternative meals?

Response:
When the school purchases and sells the product itself, the fast-food chain incurs no more obligations than any other wholesaler or retailer of food products. Consequently, it is important that parents, school food service staff, and other involved school personnel identify and discuss the particular needs of children with special needs and take steps to ensure such children, especially very young children, do not purchase "a la carte" items which can be harmful to them.

27

Technically, food items sold strictly on an "a la carte" basis are not part of a reimbursable meal. The food items are not subject to program regulations as long as they do not belong to any of the categories of foods of minimal nutritional value. The fast-food chain may not be under the obligation to provide alternate food items, unless this is explicitly stated in its contract to vend food items to the school.

However, schools would be well advised to obtain from the food chain or vendor(s) specific information on the ingredients in the food products purchased, particularly, if there are children diagnosed at risk of severe food allergies who are participating in the food service. Furthermore, the school may want to consider including such product information as a specification in its contract with the chain or vendor

D. FEEDING IN SEPARATE FACILITIES – GENERALLY NOT ACCEPTABLE

Situation 9:
A school wishes to serve meals to children with disabilities in an area separate from the cafeteria where the majority of school children eat. May the school establish a separate facility for these children?

Response:
Federal civil rights legislation, including Section 504 of the *Rehabilitation Act of 1973*, IDEA, and Title II of the ADA, requires that in providing for or arranging for the provision of nonacademic services and extracurricular activities, including meals, school districts must ensure that students with disabilities participate along with children without disabilities to the maximum extent appropriate to the needs of students with disabilities.

In general, children with disabilities must be allowed to participate with other children to the maximum extent appropriate. In this way, the child has the opportunity to interact with and learn from children without disabilities. The school must not segregate children with disabilities on the basis of convenience to the school or to other children.

In rare instances, however, it may be to a child's benefit to be served separately. For instance, a child with severe motor disabilities may be able to receive individualized attention in handling eating utensils if a special education specialist is able to work with them outside the cafeteria.

Nevertheless, it must be emphasized that in all cases, the decision to feed children with disabilities separately must always be based on what is appropriate to meet the needs of the children. Schools cannot segregate children with disabilities based on the convenience of the school or other children.

E. TEMPORARY DISABILITIES

Situation 10:
A child was involved in an accident and underwent major oral surgery. As a result, the child will be unable to consume food for a period of time unless the texture is modified. Is the school obligated to make this accommodation even though the child will not be permanently disabled?

Response:

A child's whose disability restricts their diet must be provided substitutions or modifications to foods regardless of the duration of the disability.

F. COMPLICATED FEEDINGS

Situation 11:
A child enrolled in the school will require tube feedings. Is the food service only required to pay for and provide the food, or are the costs for the school nurse, an aide or a specially trained professional to administer the feeding also assigned to the food service?

Response:
It must be emphasized that the overall responsibility for accommodating children with disabilities rests with the school district. The school district administration is responsible for allocating the district's costs of accommodating children with disabilities and for deciding which personnel will work with individual children.

In most instances involving food substitutions, the school food service account will be used to pay the cost of special food and food preparation equipment and food service personnel will generally be responsible for providing the alternate meal. For example, if a child must have a pureed meal, it is reasonable to expect the school food service to purchase a blender or food processor, and to have the meal prepared by the food service staff.

In the case of more delicate operations, such as tube feeding, it is advisable that commercial nutritive formulas, prescribed by a licensed physician, and specially designed for tube feedings, be used rather than a school blenderized formula, which may be subject to spoilage and may not always have the correct consistency or nutritive content. Proper administration of this type of feeding generally requires the skills of specially trained personnel, such as nurses or the special trained aides who regularly work with the child.

Special labor costs may be covered through special education funds, if the child has an IEP. If the child does not have an IEP, these costs may, as appropriate, be charged in part to the food service account, or may be assigned to the school district's general fund or to other funding sources.

Situation 12:
A child with a disability is on a number of medications. The physician's statement is well defined and includes menus with specific foods. If a situation arises where specific foods are out of stock, should school food service make substitutions on an "as necessary" basis?

Response:
No. School food service staff cannot decide what substitutions are appropriate for a given child. Food service staff should not choose the substitutions themselves because a child may be on a specific medication, which could interact in a negative way with a particular food item.

Ideally, a list of appropriate substitutions should accompany the menus and the foods should be on hand on a regular basis. If such a list is not available, school food service staff must ask parents to obtain from the child's physician (or the individual who planned the child's menus) a list of those foods that may be substituted.

G. SCHOOL FOOD SERVICE ACCOUNT

Situation 13:

A child with a disability needs to consume six cans of a nutritional supplement during the school day: two cans at breakfast, one can as a mid-morning snack, two cans at lunch, and one can as a mid-afternoon snack. The cost of the breakfast and lunch supplements is allowable food service expenses. If the school chooses to offer the additional supplement at the mid-morning and mid-afternoon snack period, are these allowable costs to the food service account?

Response:

Yes. While it is not required that these costs be charged to the nonprofit school food service account, these supplements are a legitimate charge to the food service account.

Situation 14:

A child with a disability requires the services of the school nurse for assistance in feeding at lunch. Can the food service account be billed for the services of non-food service personnel such as the school nurse or special aide who may be assisting in the feeding of the child or other nutrition related activity?

Response:

Yes. The services of any personnel necessary to the food service can be paid by the food service account on a pro rata basis. It must be emphasized, however, that the food service account may only pay for the amount of time that the person actually spends on activities related to the school food service. If a school nurse spends one hour per day feeding a child with a special need, then only that portion of his/her salary can be charged to the food service account, not the entire salary. If the child is receiving special education and the child's IEP includes a nutrition or feeding component, special education funds may be available to the school to provide required services for the child.

H. DOCUMENTATION

Situation 15:
The physician's statement only specifies the medical disability, not the required food substitutions. What should the food service director do?

Response:
An appropriate school official (such as the food service director, food service manager or school nurse) must ask parents to obtain more written information from the physician concerning the substitutions or modifications the child requires. If difficulties arise in obtaining the needed information, the parent(s) should be advised of the problem and asked to work with the school to obtain a complete medical statement for the child. It is important that the family understand that the school is unable to provide food substitutions or modifications without an adequate diet order or diet prescription.

In some cases, it may be appropriate and helpful for the physician to provide a written referral to a registered dietitian or other qualified professional for diet substitutions. For further guidance or referral to a registered dietitian, school food service directors may contact their State agency.

VI. SAMPLE DOCUMENTATION FOR SPECIAL DIETARY NEEDS

It is important to document the special nutritional needs of children requiring dietary modifications. Keeping a record will protect the school and minimize misunderstandings. The medical statement does not have to be renewed each year if there are no changes in the diet order. Be sure to note and date any changes in the child's medical condition or diet order.

A. EATING/FEEDING EVALUATION

Figure 1 includes a sample Eating and Feeding Evaluation: Children with Special Needs. This form should be completed by a parent, a physician, or other recognized medical authority.

B. INFORMATION CARD

Figure 2 gives an example of an information card, which can be used daily by school food service staff in the kitchen to prepare meals for the children who have special dietary or medical needs.

(The Information Card and the Eating/Feeding
Evaluation Form were adapted, with permission,
from forms developed by Susan Woods, R.D., for
Bibb County Schools in Georgia.)

FIGURE 1.   EATING AND FEEDING EVALUATION: CHILDREN WITH SPECIAL NEEDS

PART A		
Student's Name	Age	
Name of School	Grade Level	Classroom

Does the child have a disability? If Yes, describe the major life activities affected by the disability.	Yes	No
Does the child have special nutritional or feeding needs? If Yes, complete Part B of this form and have it signed by a licensed physician.	Yes	No
If the child is not disabled, does the child have special nutritional or feeding needs? If Yes, complete Part B of this form and have it signed by a recognized medical authority.	Yes	No
If the child does not require special meals, the parent can sign at the bottom and return the form to the school food service.		

PART B
List any dietary restrictions or special diet.
List any allergies or food intolerances to avoid.
List foods to be substituted.
List foods that need the following change in texture. If all foods need to be prepared in this manner, indicate "All."   Cut up or chopped into bite size pieces: Finely ground: Pureed:
List any special equipment or utensils that are needed.
Indicate any other comments about the child's eating or feeding patterns.

Parent's Signature	Date:
Physician or Medical Authority's Signature	Date:

FIGURE 2.   INFORMATION CARD

Student's Name	Teacher's Name
Special Diet or Dietary Restrictions	
Food Allergies or Intolerances	
Food Substitutions	
Foods Requiring Texture Modifications: Chopped: Finely Ground: Pureed or Blended:	
Other Diet Modifications:	
Feeding Techniques	
Supplemental Feedings	
Physician or Medical Authority: Name Telephone Fax	
Additional Contact: Name Telephone Fax	Additional Contact: Name Telephone Fax
School Food Service Representative/Person Completing Form: Title Signature	Date:

VII. GLOSSARY

AMERICANS WITH DISABILITIES ACT (ADA)
Comprehensive legislation, signed into law on July 26, 1990, that creates new rights and extends existing rights for Americans with disabilities. Title II of the Act is especially significant for the school nutrition programs, as it requires equal availability and accessibility in State and local government programs and services, including public schools.

ANAPHYLAXIS/ANAPHYLACTIC REACTION
A rare but potentially fatal condition in which several different parts of the body experience food-allergic reactions at the same time. Symptoms may progress rapidly and include severe itching, hives, sweating, swelling of the throat, breathing difficulties, lowered blood pressure, unconsciousness and even death.

DISABILITY
Under Section 504 of the *Rehabilitation Act of 1973* and the *Americans with Disabilities Act*, "person with a disability" means any person who has a physical or mental impairment which substantially limits one or more major life activities, has a record of such an impairment, or is regarded as having such an impairment. The term "physical or mental impairment" includes, but is not limited to, such diseases and conditions as orthopedic, visual, speech, and hearing impairments; cerebral palsy; epilepsy; muscular dystrophy; multiple sclerosis; cancer; heart disease; metabolic diseases such as diabetes and phenylketonuria (PKU); food anaphylaxis; mental retardation; emotional illness; and drug addiction and alcoholism. Major life activities covered by this definition include caring for one's self, eating, performing manual tasks, walking, seeing, hearing, speaking, breathing, learning and working.

Under the *Individuals with Disabilities Education Act* (IDEA), the term "disability" refers to specified physical, mental, emotional, or sense impairments, which adversely affect a child's educational performance. Thirteen recognized disability categories, which establish a child's need for special education and related services, are listed in IDEA. These disabilities include autism; deaf-blindness; deafness or other hearing impairments; mental retardation; orthopedic impairments; other health impairments due to acute health problems (such as a heart condition, epilepsy, or tuberculosis); emotional disturbance; specific learning disabilities; speech or language impairment; traumatic brain injury; visual impairment, including blindness, which adversely affects a child's educational performance.

FOOD ALLERGY

Hypersensitivity from an abnormal response of the body's immune system to food or food additives that would otherwise be considered harmless. Many of the true food allergy symptoms often resemble allergic reactions to other substances, such as penicillin, drugs, bee stings, hives and itching.

FOOD INTOLERANCE

An adverse food-induced reaction that does not involve the body's immune system. Lactose intolerance is one example of a food intolerance. A person with lactose intolerance lacks an enzyme that is needed to digest milk sugar. When milk products are consumed symptoms such as gas, bloating, and abdominal pain may occur.

FREE APPROPRIATE PUBLIC EDUCATION (FAPE)

Under the *Individuals with Disabilities Education Act*, FAPE means special education and related services provided under public supervision and direction, in conformity with an individualized education program (IEP), and at no cost to parents. In appropriate situations, nutrition services could be deemed "special education" (specially designed instruction) or a "related service" (support services required to assist a child with a disability to benefit from special education).

INDIVIDUALS WITH DISABILITIES EDUCATION ACT (IDEA)

Formerly the *Education of the Handicapped Act*, originally enacted in 1975, IDEA includes Part B, the basic grants to States program, which provides Federal funds to assist States and school districts in making a free appropriate public education available to eligible students with specified disabilities.

INDIVIDUALIZED EDUCATION PROGRAM (IEP)

The Individualized Education Program or IEP means a written statement for a child with a disability that is developed, reviewed, and revised in a meeting in accordance with the IDEA and its implementing regulations. The IEP is the cornerstone of the student's educational program that contains the program of special education and related services to be provided to a child with a disability covered under the IDEA.

NOTE: Some states supplement the IEP with a written statement specifically designed to address a student's nutritional needs. Other states employ a "Health Care Plan" to address the nutritional needs of their students. For ease of reference the term "IEP" is used to reflect the IEP as well as any written statement designating the required nutrition services.

OSTEOPATHIC PHYSICIAN OR DOCTOR OF OSTEOPATHIC MEDICINE

A fully trained physician who is licensed by the State to prescribe medication or to perform surgery. The American Medical Association includes osteopathic physicians as equal members with M.D.s. The majority of doctors of osteopathic medicine are primary care physicians.

SPECIAL DIETARY NEEDS

An individual who does not have a disability, as defined in 7 CFR 15(b), but is unable to consume a particular food because of a medical or other special dietary condition is considered to have a special dietary need. The individual's special dietary need and the needed substitution(s) must be supported by a medical statement from a licensed medical authority or other appropriate health professional as designated by the State. A person with special dietary needs may have a food allergy or intolerance (for example, lactose intolerance) but does not have life-threatening (anaphylactic) reactions when exposed to food(s) to which he/she is allergic.

RECOGNIZED MEDICAL AUTHORITY

Physicians, physician assistants, nurse practitioners; or other professionals specified by the State agency. See *FNS Instruction 783-2, Revision 2, Meal Substitutions for Medical or Other Special Dietary Reasons.*

REGISTERED DIETITIAN (R.D.)

A nutrition professional who has earned a B.S. or B.A. degree, met basic academic and clinical training requirements, and passed the qualifying examination for professional registration for dietetics. The registration program is maintained by the Commission on Dietetic Registration of the American Dietetic Association. R.D.s can answer questions on special diets, menu planning, and related topics and conduct a nutritional assessment. An R.D. may work with the physician and school staff to assist in meeting a child's special nutritional needs and to ensure that menus are in compliance with the physician's diet order.

REHABILITATION ACT OF 1973

The principal Federal legislation aimed at promoting the employment and independent living of people with disabilities. Section 504 of Title V of this legislation prohibits discrimination against qualified persons with disabilities in the programs or activities (including hiring practices) of any organization receiving Federal financial assistance.

APPENDICES

UNITED STATES DEPARTMENT OF AGRICULTURE FNS INSTRUCTION 783-2
Food and Nutrition Service REV. 2
3101 Park Center Drive
Alexandria, VA 22302

ACTION BY: Regional Directors
Special Nutrition Programs

SOURCE CITATION: Rehabilitation Act of 1973, Section 504;
7 CFR Part 15b; 7 CFR Sections 210.10(i)(1), 210.23(b),
215.14, 220.8(f), 225.16(g)(4), and 226.20(h)

Meal Substitutions for Medical
or Other Special Dietary Reasons

Child Nutrition Program regulations require participating school food authorities, institutions and sponsors to offer to all participants breakfasts, lunches, suppers, supplements and milk which meet the meal patterns identified in the Program regulations. Departmental regulations further <u>require</u> substitutions to the standard meal patterns for participants who are considered handicapped under 7 CFR Part 15b and whose handicap restricts their diet; and <u>permit</u> substitutions for other participants who are not handicapped but are unable to consume regular Program meals because of medical or other special dietary needs. The provisions requiring substitutions for handicapped participants respond to the requirements of Section 504 of the Rehabilitation Act of 1973 and to the U.S. Department of Agriculture's implementing regulations, 7 CFR Part 15b, which provide that no otherwise qualified handicapped individuals shall, solely on the basis of handicap, be excluded from participation in, be denied benefit of, or subjected to discrimination under any program or activity receiving Federal financial assistance.

This Instruction outlines the policy for food substitutions and other modifications in the meal patterns necessary to meet the dietary requirements of Program participants with handicaps and with other special dietary needs. School food authorities, institutions and sponsors are required to offer Program meals to participants with handicaps whenever Program meals are offered to the general populations served by the Programs. School food authorities, institutions and sponsors should be aware that the

DISTRIBUTION: MANUAL MAINTENANCE RESPONSIBLE FOR PAGE 1
5,6,7,11,12 INSTRUCTIONS: PREPARATION AND 10-14-94
Remove FNS Instruction 783-2, Rev. 1, MAINTENANCE:
from Manual. Insert this Instruction. CND-100

Individuals with Disabilities Education Act (IDEA) imposes requirements on States which may affect them, including the service of meals even when such service is not required by the Child Nutrition Programs.

For example, the individualized education program developed for a child under the IDEA may require a meal to be served outside of the regular meal schedule for Program meals or may require a breakfast to be served in a school food authority which does not participate in the School Breakfast Program. While the school food authority, institution or sponsor may not claim these meals as Program meals, it may use the same food service facilities or food service management company to provide these meals as it uses to provide Program meals, and Program funds may be used to pay for the costs associated with the IDEA-required meals. Inquiries regarding the IDEA's requirements should be directed to the U.S. Department of Education, the Agency responsible for the IDEA's administration and enforcement.

School food authorities, institutions and sponsors may also have responsibilities under the Americans with Disabilities Act (ADA). Inquiries regarding a school food authority's, institution's or sponsor's responsibilities under the ADA should be directed to the U.S. Department of Education, the agency responsible for the enforcement of the ADA's requirements in elementary and secondary education systems.

I   HANDICAPPED PARTICIPANTS

"Handicapped person" is defined in 7 CFR 15b.3(i) as any person who has "a physical or mental impairment which substantially limits one or more major life activities, has a record of such impairment, or is regarded as having such an impairment." (See Exhibit A, 7 CFR 15b.3.) "Major -life activities" are defined in 7 CFR 15b.3(k) as "functions such as caring for one's self, performing manual tasks, walking, seeing, hearing, speaking, breathing, learning and working." School food authorities, institutions and sponsors participating in the Child Nutrition Programs are required to make substitutions or modifications to the meal patterns for those participants with handicaps who are unable to consume the meals offered to nonhandicapped participants.

Determinations of whether or not a participant has a handicap which restricts his or her diet are to be made on an individual basis by a licensed physician. (Licensed physicians include Doctors of Osteopathy in many states.) The physician's medical statement of the participant's handicap must be based on the regulatory criteria for "handicapped person" defined in 7 CFR Part 15b.3(i) and contain a finding that the handicap restricts the participant's diet. In those cases in which the school food authority, institution or sponsor has consulted with the physician issuing the statement and is still unclear whether the medical statement meets the regulatory criteria, the school food authority, institution or sponsor may consult the State agency.

A participant whose handicap restricts his or her diet shall be provided substitutions in foods only when supported by a statement signed by a licensed physician. The medical statement shall identify:

A.   The participant's handicap and an explanation of why the handicap restricts the participant's diet;

B.   The major life activity affected by the handicap; and

C.   The food or foods to be omitted from the participant's diet, and the food or choice of foods that must be substituted.

If the handicap would require caloric modifications or the substitution of a liquid nutritive formula, for example, this information must be included in the statement. If the handicapped participant requires only textural modification(s) to the regular Program meal, as opposed to a meal pattern modification, the medical statement is recommended, but not required. In such cases, the purpose of the statement is to assist the school food authority, institution or sponsor in providing the appropriate textural modification(s). Unless otherwise specified by the physician, the meals modified for texture will consist only of food items and quantities specified in the regular menus.

The State agency should make 7 CFR 15b.3 (Exhibit A) available to school food authorities, institutions and sponsors. The school food authority, institution or sponsor should also provide parents or guardians with 7 CFR Part 15b.3, so that their physicians may correctly assess whether an individual's handicap meets the regulatory criteria. School food authorities, institutions and sponsors should use the services of a Registered Dietitian to assist in implementing the medical statement, as appropriate.

Generally, participants with food allergies or intolerances, or obese participants are not "handicapped persons", as defined in 7 CFR 15b.3(i), and school food authorities, institutions and sponsors are not required to make substitutions for them. However, when in the physician's assessment food allergies may result in severe, life-threatening reactions (anaphylactic reactions) or the obesity is severe enough to substantially limit a major life activity, the participant then meets the definition of "handicapped person", and the food service personnel must make the substitutions prescribed by the physician.

II   PARTICIPANTS WITH OTHER SPECIAL DIETARY NEEDS

School food authorities, institutions or sponsors may, at their discretion, make substitutions for individual participants who are not "handicapped persons", as defined in 7 CFR Part 15b.3(i), but who are unable to consume a food item because of medical or other special dietary needs. Such substitutions may only be made on a case-by-case basis when supported by a statement signed by a recognized medical authority. In these cases, recognized medical authorities may include physicians, physician assistants, nurse practitioners or other professionals specified by the State agency.

For these nonhandicapped participants, the supporting statement shall include:

     A.   An identification of the medical or other special dietary need which restricts the participant's diet; and

     B.   The food or foods to be omitted from the participant's diet, and the food or choice of foods that may be substituted.

School food authorities, institutions and sponsors are not required to make substitutions for participants whose conditions do not meet the definition of "handicapped person" set forth in 7 CFR 15b.3(i). For example, individuals who are overweight or have elevated blood cholesterol generally do not meet the definition of handicapped person, and thus school food authorities, institutions, and sponsors are not required to make meal substitutions for them. In fact, in most cases, the special dietary needs of nonhandicapped participants may be managed within the normal Program meal service when a well-planned variety of nutritious foods is available to children, and/or "offer versus serve" is available and implemented.

III   REIMBURSEMENT AND AVAILABILITY OF SUBSTITUTIONS

Reimbursement for meals served with an authorized substitute food to handicapped participants or to participants with other special dietary needs shall be claimed at the same reimbursement rate as meals which meet the meal pattern. Furthermore, there shall not be a supplementary charge for the substituted food item(s) to either a handicapped participant or to a participant with other special dietary needs. 7 CFR 15b.26(d)(1) specifies that, in providing food services, recipients of Federal financial assistance "may not discriminate on the basis of handicap" and "shall serve special meals, at no extra charge, to students whose handicap restricts their diet." While any additional costs for substituted foods are considered allowable Program costs, no additional Child Nutrition Program reimbursement is available. Sources of supplemental funding may include special education funds (if the substituted food is specified in the child's individualized education program); the general account of the school food authority, institution or sponsor; or, for school food authorities, the nonprofit school food service account.

IV   ACCESSIBILITY

7 CFR 15b.26(d)(2) provides: "Where existing food service facilities are not completely accessible and usable, recipients may provide aides or use other equally effective methods to serve food to handicapped persons." The school food authority, institution or sponsor is responsible for the accessibility of food service sites and for ensuring the provision of aides, where needed. As with additional costs for substituted foods, any additional costs for adaptive feeding equipment or for aides are considered allowable costs. However, no additional Child Nutrition Program reimbursement is available. Sources of supplemental funding may include special education funds (if specified in the child's individualized education program); the general account of the school food authority, institution or sponsor; or, for school food authorities, the nonprofit school food service account.

7 CFR 15b.26(d)(2) further provides that recipients provide all food services in the most integrated setting appropriate to the needs of the handicapped persons as required by 7 CFR 15b.23(b).

That section requires Program recipients to ensure that handicapped persons participate with nonhandicapped persons to the maximum extent appropriate to the needs of the handicapped person in question.

V COOPERATION

When implementing the guidelines of this Instruction, food service personnel should work closely with the parent(s) or responsible family member(s) and with all other school, child care, medical and community personnel who are responsible for the health, well-being and education of participants with handicaps or with other special dietary needs to ensure that reasonable accommodations are made to allow such individuals' participation in the meal service. This cooperation is particularly important when accommodating children or elderly adults whose handicapping conditions require significant modifications or personal assistance.

ALBERTA C. FROST
Director
Child Nutrition Division

Page 6
10-14 –94

§ 15b.3 Definitions.

As used in this part, the term or phrase:

(a) *The Act* means the Rehabilitation Act of 1973, Public Law 93–112, 87 Stat. 390 (1973), as amended by the Rehabilitation Act Amendments of 1974, Public Law 93–651, 89 Stat. 2 (1974) and Public Law 93–516, 88 Stat. 1617 (1974) and the Rehabilitation, Comprehensive Services and Developmental Disabilities Amendments of 1978, Public Law 95–602, 92 Stat. 2955 (1978). The Act appears at 29 U.S.C. 701–794.

(b) *Section 504* means section 504 of the Act, 29 U.S.C. 794.

(c) *Education of the Handicapped Act* means the Education of the Handicapped Act, Public Law 92–230, Title VI, 84 Stat. 175 (1970), as amended by the Education of the Handicapped Amendments of 1974, Public Law 93–380, Title VI, 88 Stat. 576 (1974), the Education for All Handicapped Children Act of 1975, Public Law 94–142, 89 Stat. 773 (1975), and the Education of the Handicapped Amendments of 1977, Public Law 95–49, 91 Stat. 230 (1977). The Education of the Handicapped Act appears at 20 U.S.C. 1401–1461.

(d) *Department* means the Department of Agriculture and includes each of its operating agencies and other organizational units.

(e) *Secretary* means the Secretary of Agriculture or any officer or employee of the Department to whom the Secretary has delegated or may delegate the authority to act under the regulations of this part.

(f) *Recipient* means any State or its political subdivision, any instrumentality of a State or its political subdivision, any public or private agency, institution, organization, or other entity, or any person to which Federal financial assistance is extended directly or through another recipient, including any successor, assignee, or transferee of a recipient, but excluding the ultimate beneficiary of the assistance.

(g) *Federal financial assistance* or *assistance* means any grant, contract (other than a procurement contract or a contract of insurance or guaranty), cooperative agreement, formula allocation, loan, or any other arrangement by which the Department provides or otherwise makes available assistance in the form of:

(1) Funds;

(2) Services of Federal personnel;

(3) Real and personal Federal property or any interest in Federal property, including:

(i) A sale, transfer, lease or use (on other than a casual or transient basis) of Federal property for less than fair market value, for reduced consideration or in recognition of the public nature of the recipient's program or activity; and

(ii) Proceeds from a subsequent sale, transfer or lease of Federal property if the Federal share of its fair market value is not returned to the Federal Government.

(4) Any other thing of value.

(h) *Facility* means all or any portion of buildings, structures, equipment, roads, walks, parking lots, or other real or personal property or interest in such property.

(i) *Handicapped person* means any person who has a physical or mental impairment which substantially limits one or more major life activities, has a record of such an impairment, or is regarded as having such an impairment.

(j) *Physical or mental impairment* means (1) any physiological disorder or condition, cosmetic disfigurement, or anatomical loss affecting one or more of the following body systems: Neurological; musculoskeletal; special sense organs; respiratory, including speech organs; cardiovascular; reproductive; digestive; genitourinary; hemic and lymphatic; skin; and endocrine; or (2) any mental or psychological disorder, such as mental retardation, organic brain syndrome, emotional or mental illness, and specific learning disabilities. The term *physical or mental impairment* includes, but is not limited to, such diseases and conditions as orthopedic, visual, speech, and hearing impairments; cerebral palsy; epilepsy;

muscular dystrophy; multiple sclerosis, cancer; heart disease; diabetes; mental retardation; emotional illness; and drug addiction and alcoholism.

(k) *Major life activities* means functions such as caring for one's self, performing manual tasks, walking, seeing, hearing, speaking, breathing, learning and working.

(1) *Has a record of such an impairment* means has a history of, or has been misclassified as having, a mental or physical impairment that substantially limits one or more major life activities.

(m) *Is regarded as having an impairment* means (1) has a physical or mental impairment that does not substantially limit major life activities but that is treated by a recipient as constituting such a limitation; (2) has a physical or mental impairment that substantially limits major life activities only as a result of the attitudes of others towards such impairments, or (3) has none of the impairments defined in paragraph (j) of this section but is treated by a recipient as having such an impairment.

(n) *Qualified handicapped person* (used synonymously with *otherwise qualified handicapped individual*) means:

(1) With respect to employment, a handicapped person who, with reasonable accommodation, can perform the essential functions of the job in question, but the term does not include any individual who is an alcoholic or drug abuser whose current use of alcohol or drugs prevents such individual from performing the duties of the job in question or whose employment, by reason of such current alcohol or drug abuse, would constitute a direct threat to property or the safety of others;

(2) With respect to public preschool, elementary, secondary, or adult educational services, a handicapped person, (i) of an age during which non-handicapped persons are provided such services, (ii) of an age during which it is mandatory under State law to provide such services to handicapped persons, or (iii) to whom a State is required to provide a free appropriate public education under section 612 of the Education of the Handicapped Act; and

(3) With respect to postsecondary and vocational education services, a handicapped person who meets all academic and technical standards requisite to admission or participation in the recipient's education program or activity;

(4) With respect to other services, a handicapped person who meets the essential eligibility requirements for the receipt of such services.

(o) *Handicap* means any condition or characteristic that renders a person a handicapped person as defined in paragraph (i) of this section.

(p) For purposes of § 15b.18(d), *Historic preservation programs* means programs receiving Federal financial assistance that has preservation of historic properties as a primary purpose.

(q) For purposes of § 15b.18(e), *Historic properties* means those buildings or facilities that are eligible for listing in the National Register of Historic Places, or such properties designated as historic under a statute of the appropriate State or local government body.

(r) For purposes of § 15b.18(d), *Substantial impairment* means a significant loss of the integrity of finished materials, design quality or special character which loss results from a permanent alteration.

[47 FR 25470, June 11, 1982, as amended at 55 FR 52139, Dec. 19, 1990]

USDA, Food and Nutrition Service
Regional Directors

Regional Director Mid-Atlantic Regional Office (MARO), USDA, FNS, SNP Mercer Corporate Park 300 Corporate Boulevard Robbinsville, NJ 08691-1598 609-259-5025	Mid-Atlantic Regional States Delaware, Virginia, District of Columbia, Virgin Islands, Maryland, West Virginia, New Jersey, Pennsylvania, Puerto Rico
Regional Director Midwest Regional Office (MWRO), USDA, FNS, SNP 77 West Jackson Blvd 20th Floor Chicago, IL 60604-3507 312-353-6664	Midwest Regional States Illinois, Indiana, Michigan, Minnesota, Ohio Wisconsin
Regional Director Mountain Plains Regional Office (MPRO), USDA, FNS, SNP 1244 Speer Boulevard Suite 903 Denver, CO 80204 303-844-0300	Mountain Plains Regional States Colorado, South Dakota, Iowa, North Dakota, Kansas, Utah, Missouri, Wyoming, Montana Nebraska
Regional Director Northeast Regional Office (NERO), USDA, FNS, SNP 10 Causeway Street Room 501 Boston, MA 02222-1065 617-565-6370	Northeast Regional States Connecticut, Vermont, Maine, Massachusetts, New Hampshire, New York, Rhode Island
Regional Director Southeast Regional Office (SERO), USDA, FNS, SNP 61 Forsyth Street, SW Room 8T36 Atlanta, GA 30303 404-562-1800	Southeast Regional States Alabama, South Carolina, Florida, Georgia, Kentucky, Tennessee, Mississippi, North Carolina
Regional Director Southwest Regional Office (SWRO), USDA, FNS, SNP 1100 Commerce Street Room 5C30 Dallas, TX 75242 214-290-9800	Southwest Regional States Arkansas, Louisiana, New Mexico, Oklahoma, Texas
Regional Director Western Regional Office (WRO), USDA, FNS, SNP 550 Kearny Street Room 400 San Francisco, CA 94108 415-705-2229	Western Regional States Alaska, Oregon, American Samoa, Arizona, Washington, California, Guam, Hawaii, Trust Territories, Idaho, Nevada, Commonwealth of the Northern Mariana Islands

Regional Civil Rights Offices

Regional Director MARO Civil Rights Mercer Corporate Park 300 Corporate Boulevard Robbinsville, NJ 08691-1598 609-259-5123	Mid-Atlantic Regional States Delaware, Virginia, District of Columbia, Virgin Islands, Maryland, West Virginia, New Jersey, Puerto Rico, Pennsylvania
Regional Director MWRO Civil Rights 77 West Jackson Blvd 20th Floor Chicago, IL 60604-3507 312-353-3353	Midwest Regional States: Illinois, Wisconsin, Indiana, Michigan, Minnesota, Ohio
Regional Director MPRO Civil Rights 1244 Speer Boulevard Suite 903 Denver, CO 80204 303-844-0307	Mountain Plains Regional States: Colorado, South Dakota, Iowa, North Dakota, Kansas, Utah, Missouri, Wyoming, Montana, Nebraska
Regional Director NERO Civil Rights 10 Causeway Street Room 501 Boston, MA 02222-1065 617-565-6424	Northeast Regional States Connecticut, Vermont, Maine, Rhode Island, Massachusetts, New Hampshire, New York
Regional Director SERO Civil Rights 61 Forsyth Street, SW Room 8t36 Atlanta, GA 30303 404-562-1808	Southeast Regional States: Alabama, South Carolina, Florida, Georgia, Kentucky, Tennessee, Mississippi, North Carolina
Regional Director SWRO Civil Rights 1100 Commerce Street Room 5-A-6 Dallas, TX 75242 214-290-9820	Southwest Regional States: Arkansas, Louisiana, New Mexico, Oklahoma, Texas
Regional Director WRO Civil Rights 550 Kearny Street Room 400 San Francisco, CA 94108 415-705-1322	Western Regional States: Alaska, Oregon, American Samoa, Arizona, Washington, California, Guam, Hawaii, Trust Territories, Idaho, Nevada, Commonwealth of the Northern Mariana Islands

U.S. Department of Health and Human Services
Regional Contacts

Region I
Connecticut, Maine Massachusetts, New Hampshire, Rhode Island, Vermont
Boston Regional Office
John F. Kennedy Federal Building
Boston, MA 02203-0003
Medicaid Associate Regional Administrator   617-565-1223
EPSDT and MCH Regional Coordinator   617-565-1243

Region II
New Jersey, New York Puerto Rico, Virgin Islands
New York Regional Office
26 Federal Plaza, Room 3800
New York, NY 10278-0063
Medicaid Associate Regional Administrator   212-264-2058
EPSDT and MCH Regional Coordinator   212-264-3978

Region III
Delaware, District of Columbia, Maryland, Pennsylvania, Virginia, West Virginia
Philadelphia Regional Office
The Public Ledger Building
150 South Independence Mall West
Philadelphia, PA 19106
Medicaid Associate Regional Administrator (EPSDT)   215-861-4220
MCH Regional Coordinator   215-861-4252

Region IV
Alabama, Florida, Georgia, Kentucky, Mississippi, North Carolina, South
Carolina, Tennessee
Atlanta Regional Office
Atlanta Federal Center,Suite 4T20
61 Forsyth Street, SW
Atlanta, GA 30303-8909
Medicaid Associate Regional Administrator   404-562-7401
EPSDT and MCH Regional Coordinator   404-562-7465

U.S. Department of Health and Human Services
Regional Contacts

Region V
Illinois, Indiana, Michigan, Minnesota, Ohio, Wisconsin
Chicago Regional Office
233 N. Michigan Ave., Suite 600
Chicago, IL 60601-5519
Medicaid Associate Regional Administrator   312-353-2702
EPSDT and MCH Regional Coordinator   312-353-3721

Region VI
Arkansas, Louisiana, New Mexico, Oklahoma, Texas
Dallas Regional Office
1301 Young St. Room 833, 8th. Fl.
Dallas, TX 75202
Medicaid Associate Regional Administrator   214-767-6301
EPSDT and MCH Regional Coordinator   214-767-6497

Region VII
Iowa, Kansas, Missouri, Nebraska
Kansas City Regional Office
Richard Bolling Federal Building
601 East 12th Street
Kansas City, MO 64106-2808
Medicaid Associate Regional Administrator   816-426-5925
EPSDT and MCH Regional Coordinator   816-426-3406

Region VIII
Colorado, Montana, North Dakota, South Dakota, Utah, Wyoming
Denver Regional Office
Health Care Finance Administration
Division of Medicaid and State Operations
1600 Broadway, Suite 700
Denver, CO 80202
Medicaid Associate Regional Administrator   303-844-1977
EPSDT and MCH Regional Coordinator   303-844-2682

U.S. Department of Health and Human Services
Regional Contacts

Region IX
American Samoa, Arizona, CNMI, Guam, California, Hawaii, Nevada
San Francisco Regional Office
75 Hawthorne Street
San Francisco, CA 94105-3901
Medicaid Associate Regional Administrator   415-744-3568
EPSDT Regional Coordinator   415-744-3596

Regional MCH Program Consultant
Federal Office Building
50 United Nations Plaza
San Francisco, CA 94102   415-744-3553

Region X
Alaska, Idaho, Oregon, Washington,
Seattle Regional Office
2201 Sixth Avenue
Seattle, WA 98121-2500
Medicaid Associate Regional Administrator   206-615-2313
EPSDT and MCH Regional Coordinator   206-615-2343

Voluntary and Professional
Health Organizations

American Academy of Allergy,
Asthma, and Immunology
1-800-822-2762
www.aaaai.org

American Academy of Pediatrics
1-847-434-4000 (National
Headquarters)
www.aap.org

American Cancer Society
1-800-ACS-2345
www.cancer.org

American Diabetes Association
1-800-DIABETES
www.diabetes.org

American Heart Association
1-800-AHA-USA1
www.americanheart.org

Arthritis Foundation
1-800-283-7800
www.arthritis. org

Association for Retarded Citizens
(The ARC)
National Headquarters
301-565-3842
www.thearc.org

Autism Society of America
1-800-3-AUTISM
www.autism-society.org

Crohn's and Colitis Foundation
of America, Inc.
1-800-343-3637
www.ccfa.org

Cleft Palate Foundation
1-800-24-CLEFT
www.cleft.com

Easter Seals
312-726-6200 (voice)
312-726-4258 (TTY)
www.easter-seals.org

Epilepsy Foundation of America
1-800-EFA-1000
www.efa.org

Food Allergy & Anaphylaxis Network,
Inc.
1-800-929-4040
www.foodallergy.org

Muscular Dystrophy Association of
America
1-800-572-1717
www.mdausa.org

National Cystic Fibrosis Foundation
1-800-FIGHT CF
www.cff.org

Spina Bifida Association
of America
1-800-621-3141
www.sbaa.org

United Cerebral Palsy Association
1-800-USA5-UCP
(TTY)202-973-7197
www.ucpa.org

www.ingramcontent.com/pod-product-compliance
Lightning Source LLC
Chambersburg PA
CBHW080441290526
45791CB00008BA/2572